THIS BOOK BELONGS TO:

CONTACT INFORMATION

NAME:	
ADDRESS:	
PHONE:	

START / END DATES

_____ / / _____   TO   _____ / / _____

Dedication

This Screen Time Log Journal is dedicated to all the parents out there who want to monitor & record their kids' screen time and document their findings in the process.

You are my inspiration for producing books and I'm honored to be a part of keeping all of your screen time notes and records organized.

This journal notebook will help you record the details of your child's screen time.

Thoughtfully put together with these sections to record: Name, Week of, Devices, Monday- Sunday Tracker, Total Screen Time, How Did You Do This Week?

How to Use this Book

The purpose of this book is to keep all of your Screen Time notes all in one place. It will help keep you organized.

This Screen Time Log Journal will allow you to accurately document every detail about your child's weekly screen time.

Here are examples of the prompts for you to fill in and write about your experience in this book:

1. Name - Write the name.

2. Week Of - Record which week it is.

3. Devices - Track screen time for Cell Phone, Video Games, Tablet, Kindle, Laptop/ Computer, & TV.

4. Monday - Sunday Tracker - Log your screen time for each device for each day of the week.

5. Total Screen Time - Add up each day's total screen time spent.

6. How Did You Do This Week? - Write how you think you did this week and what you can do to improve.

Spending Screen Time

NAME	
WEEK OF	

DEVICES	MONDAY	TUESDAY	WEDNESDAY	THURSDAY	FRIDAY	SATURDAY	SUNDAY
CELL PHONE							
VIDEO GAMES							
TABLET							
KINDLE							
LAPTOP / COMPUTER							
TV							
TOTAL SCREEN TIME							

HOW DID YOU DO THIS WEEK?

Spending Screen Time

NAME	
WEEK OF	

DEVICES	MONDAY	TUESDAY	WEDNESDAY	THURSDAY	FRIDAY	SATURDAY	SUNDAY
CELL PHONE							
VIDEO GAMES							
TABLET							
KINDLE							
LAPTOP / COMPUTER							
TV							
TOTAL SCREEN TIME							

HOW DID YOU DO THIS WEEK?

Spending Screen Time

NAME	
WEEK OF	

DEVICES	MONDAY	TUESDAY	WEDNESDAY	THURSDAY	FRIDAY	SATURDAY	SUNDAY
CELL PHONE							
VIDEO GAMES							
TABLET							
KINDLE							
LAPTOP / COMPUTER							
TV							
TOTAL SCREEN TIME							

HOW DID YOU DO THIS WEEK?

Spending Screen Time

NAME	
WEEK OF	

DEVICES	MONDAY	TUESDAY	WEDNESDAY	THURSDAY	FRIDAY	SATURDAY	SUNDAY
CELL PHONE							
VIDEO GAMES							
TABLET							
KINDLE							
LAPTOP / COMPUTER							
TV							
TOTAL SCREEN TIME							

HOW DID YOU DO THIS WEEK?

Spending Screen Time

NAME	
WEEK OF	

DEVICES	MONDAY	TUESDAY	WEDNESDAY	THURSDAY	FRIDAY	SATURDAY	SUNDAY
CELL PHONE							
VIDEO GAMES							
TABLET							
KINDLE							
LAPTOP / COMPUTER							
TV							
TOTAL SCREEN TIME							

HOW DID YOU DO THIS WEEK?

Spending Screen Time

NAME	
WEEK OF	

DEVICES	MONDAY	TUESDAY	WEDNESDAY	THURSDAY	FRIDAY	SATURDAY	SUNDAY
CELL PHONE							
VIDEO GAMES							
TABLET							
KINDLE							
LAPTOP / COMPUTER							
TV							
TOTAL SCREEN TIME							

HOW DID YOU DO THIS WEEK?

Spending Screen Time

NAME	
WEEK OF	

DEVICES	MONDAY	TUESDAY	WEDNESDAY	THURSDAY	FRIDAY	SATURDAY	SUNDAY
CELL PHONE							
VIDEO GAMES							
TABLET							
KINDLE							
LAPTOP / COMPUTER							
TV							
TOTAL SCREEN TIME							

HOW DID YOU DO THIS WEEK?

Spending Screen Time

NAME	
WEEK OF	

DEVICES	MONDAY	TUESDAY	WEDNESDAY	THURSDAY	FRIDAY	SATURDAY	SUNDAY
CELL PHONE							
VIDEO GAMES							
TABLET							
KINDLE							
LAPTOP / COMPUTER							
TV							
TOTAL SCREEN TIME							

HOW DID YOU DO THIS WEEK?

Spending Screen Time

NAME	
WEEK OF	

DEVICES	MONDAY	TUESDAY	WEDNESDAY	THURSDAY	FRIDAY	SATURDAY	SUNDAY
CELL PHONE							
VIDEO GAMES							
TABLET							
KINDLE							
LAPTOP / COMPUTER							
TV							
TOTAL SCREEN TIME							

HOW DID YOU DO THIS WEEK?

Spending Screen Time

NAME	
WEEK OF	

DEVICES	MONDAY	TUESDAY	WEDNESDAY	THURSDAY	FRIDAY	SATURDAY	SUNDAY
CELL PHONE							
VIDEO GAMES							
TABLET							
KINDLE							
LAPTOP / COMPUTER							
TV							
TOTAL SCREEN TIME							

HOW DID YOU DO THIS WEEK?

Spending Screen Time

NAME	
WEEK OF	

DEVICES	MONDAY	TUESDAY	WEDNESDAY	THURSDAY	FRIDAY	SATURDAY	SUNDAY
CELL PHONE							
VIDEO GAMES							
TABLET							
KINDLE							
LAPTOP / COMPUTER							
TV							
TOTAL SCREEN TIME							

HOW DID YOU DO THIS WEEK?

Spending Screen Time

NAME	
WEEK OF	

DEVICES	MONDAY	TUESDAY	WEDNESDAY	THURSDAY	FRIDAY	SATURDAY	SUNDAY
CELL PHONE							
VIDEO GAMES							
TABLET							
KINDLE							
LAPTOP / COMPUTER							
TV							
TOTAL SCREEN TIME							

HOW DID YOU DO THIS WEEK?

Spending Screen Time

NAME	
WEEK OF	

DEVICES	MONDAY	TUESDAY	WEDNESDAY	THURSDAY	FRIDAY	SATURDAY	SUNDAY
CELL PHONE							
VIDEO GAMES							
TABLET							
KINDLE							
LAPTOP / COMPUTER							
TV							
TOTAL SCREEN TIME							

HOW DID YOU DO THIS WEEK?

Spending Screen Time

NAME	
WEEK OF	

DEVICES	MONDAY	TUESDAY	WEDNESDAY	THURSDAY	FRIDAY	SATURDAY	SUNDAY
CELL PHONE							
VIDEO GAMES							
TABLET							
KINDLE							
LAPTOP / COMPUTER							
TV							
TOTAL SCREEN TIME							

HOW DID YOU DO THIS WEEK?

Spending Screen Time

NAME	
WEEK OF	

DEVICES	MONDAY	TUESDAY	WEDNESDAY	THURSDAY	FRIDAY	SATURDAY	SUNDAY
CELL PHONE							
VIDEO GAMES							
TABLET							
KINDLE							
LAPTOP / COMPUTER							
TV							
TOTAL SCREEN TIME							

HOW DID YOU DO THIS WEEK?

Spending Screen Time

NAME		
WEEK OF		

DEVICES	MONDAY	TUESDAY	WEDNESDAY	THURSDAY	FRIDAY	SATURDAY	SUNDAY
CELL PHONE							
VIDEO GAMES							
TABLET							
KINDLE							
LAPTOP / COMPUTER							
TV							
TOTAL SCREEN TIME							

HOW DID YOU DO THIS WEEK?

Spending Screen Time

NAME	
WEEK OF	

DEVICES	MONDAY	TUESDAY	WEDNESDAY	THURSDAY	FRIDAY	SATURDAY	SUNDAY
CELL PHONE							
VIDEO GAMES							
TABLET							
KINDLE							
LAPTOP / COMPUTER							
TV							
TOTAL SCREEN TIME							

HOW DID YOU DO THIS WEEK?

Spending Screen Time

NAME	
WEEK OF	

DEVICES	MONDAY	TUESDAY	WEDNESDAY	THURSDAY	FRIDAY	SATURDAY	SUNDAY
CELL PHONE							
VIDEO GAMES							
TABLET							
KINDLE							
LAPTOP / COMPUTER							
TV							
TOTAL SCREEN TIME							

HOW DID YOU DO THIS WEEK?

Spending Screen Time

NAME	
WEEK OF	

DEVICES	MONDAY	TUESDAY	WEDNESDAY	THURSDAY	FRIDAY	SATURDAY	SUNDAY
CELL PHONE							
VIDEO GAMES							
TABLET							
KINDLE							
LAPTOP / COMPUTER							
TV							
TOTAL SCREEN TIME							

HOW DID YOU DO THIS WEEK?

Spending Screen Time

NAME	
WEEK OF	

DEVICES	MONDAY	TUESDAY	WEDNESDAY	THURSDAY	FRIDAY	SATURDAY	SUNDAY
CELL PHONE							
VIDEO GAMES							
TABLET							
KINDLE							
LAPTOP / COMPUTER							
TV							
TOTAL SCREEN TIME							

HOW DID YOU DO THIS WEEK?

Spending Screen Time

NAME	
WEEK OF	

DEVICES	MONDAY	TUESDAY	WEDNESDAY	THURSDAY	FRIDAY	SATURDAY	SUNDAY
CELL PHONE							
VIDEO GAMES							
TABLET							
KINDLE							
LAPTOP / COMPUTER							
TV							
TOTAL SCREEN TIME							

HOW DID YOU DO THIS WEEK?

Spending Screen Time

NAME	
WEEK OF	

DEVICES	MONDAY	TUESDAY	WEDNESDAY	THURSDAY	FRIDAY	SATURDAY	SUNDAY
CELL PHONE							
VIDEO GAMES							
TABLET							
KINDLE							
LAPTOP / COMPUTER							
TV							
TOTAL SCREEN TIME							

HOW DID YOU DO THIS WEEK?

Spending Screen Time

NAME		
WEEK OF		

DEVICES	MONDAY	TUESDAY	WEDNESDAY	THURSDAY	FRIDAY	SATURDAY	SUNDAY
CELL PHONE							
VIDEO GAMES							
TABLET							
KINDLE							
LAPTOP / COMPUTER							
TV							
TOTAL SCREEN TIME							

HOW DID YOU DO THIS WEEK?

Spending Screen Time

NAME	
WEEK OF	

DEVICES	MONDAY	TUESDAY	WEDNESDAY	THURSDAY	FRIDAY	SATURDAY	SUNDAY
CELL PHONE							
VIDEO GAMES							
TABLET							
KINDLE							
LAPTOP / COMPUTER							
TV							
TOTAL SCREEN TIME							

HOW DID YOU DO THIS WEEK?

Spending Screen Time

NAME	
WEEK OF	

DEVICES	MONDAY	TUESDAY	WEDNESDAY	THURSDAY	FRIDAY	SATURDAY	SUNDAY
CELL PHONE							
VIDEO GAMES							
TABLET							
KINDLE							
LAPTOP / COMPUTER							
TV							
TOTAL SCREEN TIME							

HOW DID YOU DO THIS WEEK?

Spending Screen Time

NAME	
WEEK OF	

DEVICES	MONDAY	TUESDAY	WEDNESDAY	THURSDAY	FRIDAY	SATURDAY	SUNDAY
CELL PHONE							
VIDEO GAMES							
TABLET							
KINDLE							
LAPTOP / COMPUTER							
TV							
TOTAL SCREEN TIME							

HOW DID YOU DO THIS WEEK?

Spending Screen Time

NAME	
WEEK OF	

DEVICES	MONDAY	TUESDAY	WEDNESDAY	THURSDAY	FRIDAY	SATURDAY	SUNDAY
CELL PHONE							
VIDEO GAMES							
TABLET							
KINDLE							
LAPTOP / COMPUTER							
TV							
TOTAL SCREEN TIME							

HOW DID YOU DO THIS WEEK?

Spending Screen Time

NAME	
WEEK OF	

DEVICES	MONDAY	TUESDAY	WEDNESDAY	THURSDAY	FRIDAY	SATURDAY	SUNDAY
CELL PHONE							
VIDEO GAMES							
TABLET							
KINDLE							
LAPTOP / COMPUTER							
TV							
TOTAL SCREEN TIME							

HOW DID YOU DO THIS WEEK?

Spending Screen Time

NAME	
WEEK OF	

DEVICES	MONDAY	TUESDAY	WEDNESDAY	THURSDAY	FRIDAY	SATURDAY	SUNDAY
CELL PHONE							
VIDEO GAMES							
TABLET							
KINDLE							
LAPTOP / COMPUTER							
TV							
TOTAL SCREEN TIME							

HOW DID YOU DO THIS WEEK?

Spending Screen Time

NAME	
WEEK OF	

DEVICES	MONDAY	TUESDAY	WEDNESDAY	THURSDAY	FRIDAY	SATURDAY	SUNDAY
CELL PHONE							
VIDEO GAMES							
TABLET							
KINDLE							
LAPTOP / COMPUTER							
TV							
TOTAL SCREEN TIME							

HOW DID YOU DO THIS WEEK?

Spending Screen Time

NAME	
WEEK OF	

DEVICES	MONDAY	TUESDAY	WEDNESDAY	THURSDAY	FRIDAY	SATURDAY	SUNDAY
CELL PHONE							
VIDEO GAMES							
TABLET							
KINDLE							
LAPTOP / COMPUTER							
TV							
TOTAL SCREEN TIME							

HOW DID YOU DO THIS WEEK?

Spending Screen Time

NAME	
WEEK OF	

DEVICES	MONDAY	TUESDAY	WEDNESDAY	THURSDAY	FRIDAY	SATURDAY	SUNDAY
CELL PHONE							
VIDEO GAMES							
TABLET							
KINDLE							
LAPTOP / COMPUTER							
TV							
TOTAL SCREEN TIME							

HOW DID YOU DO THIS WEEK?

Spending Screen Time

NAME	
WEEK OF	

DEVICES	MONDAY	TUESDAY	WEDNESDAY	THURSDAY	FRIDAY	SATURDAY	SUNDAY
CELL PHONE							
VIDEO GAMES							
TABLET							
KINDLE							
LAPTOP / COMPUTER							
TV							
TOTAL SCREEN TIME							

HOW DID YOU DO THIS WEEK?

Spending Screen Time

NAME	
WEEK OF	

DEVICES	MONDAY	TUESDAY	WEDNESDAY	THURSDAY	FRIDAY	SATURDAY	SUNDAY
CELL PHONE							
VIDEO GAMES							
TABLET							
KINDLE							
LAPTOP / COMPUTER							
TV							
TOTAL SCREEN TIME							

HOW DID YOU DO THIS WEEK?

Spending Screen Time

NAME	
WEEK OF	

DEVICES	MONDAY	TUESDAY	WEDNESDAY	THURSDAY	FRIDAY	SATURDAY	SUNDAY
CELL PHONE							
VIDEO GAMES							
TABLET							
KINDLE							
LAPTOP / COMPUTER							
TV							
TOTAL SCREEN TIME							

HOW DID YOU DO THIS WEEK?

Spending Screen Time

NAME	
WEEK OF	

DEVICES	MONDAY	TUESDAY	WEDNESDAY	THURSDAY	FRIDAY	SATURDAY	SUNDAY
CELL PHONE							
VIDEO GAMES							
TABLET							
KINDLE							
LAPTOP / COMPUTER							
TV							
TOTAL SCREEN TIME							

HOW DID YOU DO THIS WEEK?

Spending Screen Time

NAME		
WEEK OF		

DEVICES	MONDAY	TUESDAY	WEDNESDAY	THURSDAY	FRIDAY	SATURDAY	SUNDAY
CELL PHONE							
VIDEO GAMES							
TABLET							
KINDLE							
LAPTOP / COMPUTER							
TV							
TOTAL SCREEN TIME							

HOW DID YOU DO THIS WEEK?

Spending Screen Time

NAME	
WEEK OF	

DEVICES	MONDAY	TUESDAY	WEDNESDAY	THURSDAY	FRIDAY	SATURDAY	SUNDAY
CELL PHONE							
VIDEO GAMES							
TABLET							
KINDLE							
LAPTOP / COMPUTER							
TV							
TOTAL SCREEN TIME							

HOW DID YOU DO THIS WEEK?

Spending Screen Time

NAME	
WEEK OF	

DEVICES	MONDAY	TUESDAY	WEDNESDAY	THURSDAY	FRIDAY	SATURDAY	SUNDAY
CELL PHONE							
VIDEO GAMES							
TABLET							
KINDLE							
LAPTOP / COMPUTER							
TV							
TOTAL SCREEN TIME							

HOW DID YOU DO THIS WEEK?

Spending Screen Time

NAME	
WEEK OF	

DEVICES	MONDAY	TUESDAY	WEDNESDAY	THURSDAY	FRIDAY	SATURDAY	SUNDAY
CELL PHONE							
VIDEO GAMES							
TABLET							
KINDLE							
LAPTOP / COMPUTER							
TV							
TOTAL SCREEN TIME							

HOW DID YOU DO THIS WEEK?

Spending Screen Time

NAME	
WEEK OF	

DEVICES	MONDAY	TUESDAY	WEDNESDAY	THURSDAY	FRIDAY	SATURDAY	SUNDAY
CELL PHONE							
VIDEO GAMES							
TABLET							
KINDLE							
LAPTOP / COMPUTER							
TV							
TOTAL SCREEN TIME							

HOW DID YOU DO THIS WEEK?

Spending Screen Time

NAME	
WEEK OF	

DEVICES	MONDAY	TUESDAY	WEDNESDAY	THURSDAY	FRIDAY	SATURDAY	SUNDAY
CELL PHONE							
VIDEO GAMES							
TABLET							
KINDLE							
LAPTOP / COMPUTER							
TV							
TOTAL SCREEN TIME							

HOW DID YOU DO THIS WEEK?

Spending Screen Time

NAME	
WEEK OF	

DEVICES	MONDAY	TUESDAY	WEDNESDAY	THURSDAY	FRIDAY	SATURDAY	SUNDAY
CELL PHONE							
VIDEO GAMES							
TABLET							
KINDLE							
LAPTOP / COMPUTER							
TV							
TOTAL SCREEN TIME							

HOW DID YOU DO THIS WEEK?

Spending Screen Time

NAME	
WEEK OF	

DEVICES	MONDAY	TUESDAY	WEDNESDAY	THURSDAY	FRIDAY	SATURDAY	SUNDAY
CELL PHONE							
VIDEO GAMES							
TABLET							
KINDLE							
LAPTOP / COMPUTER							
TV							
TOTAL SCREEN TIME							

HOW DID YOU DO THIS WEEK?

Spending Screen Time

NAME	
WEEK OF	

DEVICES	MONDAY	TUESDAY	WEDNESDAY	THURSDAY	FRIDAY	SATURDAY	SUNDAY
CELL PHONE							
VIDEO GAMES							
TABLET							
KINDLE							
LAPTOP / COMPUTER							
TV							
TOTAL SCREEN TIME							

HOW DID YOU DO THIS WEEK?

Spending Screen Time

NAME	
WEEK OF	

DEVICES	MONDAY	TUESDAY	WEDNESDAY	THURSDAY	FRIDAY	SATURDAY	SUNDAY
CELL PHONE							
VIDEO GAMES							
TABLET							
KINDLE							
LAPTOP / COMPUTER							
TV							
TOTAL SCREEN TIME							

HOW DID YOU DO THIS WEEK?

Spending Screen Time

NAME	
WEEK OF	

DEVICES	MONDAY	TUESDAY	WEDNESDAY	THURSDAY	FRIDAY	SATURDAY	SUNDAY
CELL PHONE							
VIDEO GAMES							
TABLET							
KINDLE							
LAPTOP / COMPUTER							
TV							
TOTAL SCREEN TIME							

HOW DID YOU DO THIS WEEK?

Spending Screen Time

NAME	
WEEK OF	

DEVICES	MONDAY	TUESDAY	WEDNESDAY	THURSDAY	FRIDAY	SATURDAY	SUNDAY
CELL PHONE							
VIDEO GAMES							
TABLET							
KINDLE							
LAPTOP / COMPUTER							
TV							
TOTAL SCREEN TIME							

HOW DID YOU DO THIS WEEK?

Spending Screen Time

NAME	
WEEK OF	

DEVICES	MONDAY	TUESDAY	WEDNESDAY	THURSDAY	FRIDAY	SATURDAY	SUNDAY
CELL PHONE							
VIDEO GAMES							
TABLET							
KINDLE							
LAPTOP / COMPUTER							
TV							
TOTAL SCREEN TIME							

HOW DID YOU DO THIS WEEK?

Spending Screen Time

NAME	
WEEK OF	

DEVICES	MONDAY	TUESDAY	WEDNESDAY	THURSDAY	FRIDAY	SATURDAY	SUNDAY
CELL PHONE							
VIDEO GAMES							
TABLET							
KINDLE							
LAPTOP / COMPUTER							
TV							
TOTAL SCREEN TIME							

HOW DID YOU DO THIS WEEK?

Spending Screen Time

NAME	
WEEK OF	

DEVICES	MONDAY	TUESDAY	WEDNESDAY	THURSDAY	FRIDAY	SATURDAY	SUNDAY
CELL PHONE							
VIDEO GAMES							
TABLET							
KINDLE							
LAPTOP / COMPUTER							
TV							
TOTAL SCREEN TIME							

HOW DID YOU DO THIS WEEK?

Spending Screen Time

NAME	
WEEK OF	

DEVICES	MONDAY	TUESDAY	WEDNESDAY	THURSDAY	FRIDAY	SATURDAY	SUNDAY
CELL PHONE							
VIDEO GAMES							
TABLET							
KINDLE							
LAPTOP / COMPUTER							
TV							
TOTAL SCREEN TIME							

HOW DID YOU DO THIS WEEK?

Spending Screen Time

NAME	
WEEK OF	

DEVICES	MONDAY	TUESDAY	WEDNESDAY	THURSDAY	FRIDAY	SATURDAY	SUNDAY
CELL PHONE							
VIDEO GAMES							
TABLET							
KINDLE							
LAPTOP / COMPUTER							
TV							
TOTAL SCREEN TIME							

HOW DID YOU DO THIS WEEK?

Spending Screen Time

NAME	
WEEK OF	

DEVICES	MONDAY	TUESDAY	WEDNESDAY	THURSDAY	FRIDAY	SATURDAY	SUNDAY
CELL PHONE							
VIDEO GAMES							
TABLET							
KINDLE							
LAPTOP / COMPUTER							
TV							
TOTAL SCREEN TIME							

HOW DID YOU DO THIS WEEK?

Spending Screen Time

NAME	
WEEK OF	

DEVICES	MONDAY	TUESDAY	WEDNESDAY	THURSDAY	FRIDAY	SATURDAY	SUNDAY
CELL PHONE							
VIDEO GAMES							
TABLET							
KINDLE							
LAPTOP / COMPUTER							
TV							
TOTAL SCREEN TIME							

HOW DID YOU DO THIS WEEK?

Spending Screen Time

NAME	
WEEK OF	

DEVICES	MONDAY	TUESDAY	WEDNESDAY	THURSDAY	FRIDAY	SATURDAY	SUNDAY
CELL PHONE							
VIDEO GAMES							
TABLET							
KINDLE							
LAPTOP / COMPUTER							
TV							
TOTAL SCREEN TIME							

HOW DID YOU DO THIS WEEK?

Spending Screen Time

NAME	
WEEK OF	

DEVICES	MONDAY	TUESDAY	WEDNESDAY	THURSDAY	FRIDAY	SATURDAY	SUNDAY
CELL PHONE							
VIDEO GAMES							
TABLET							
KINDLE							
LAPTOP / COMPUTER							
TV							
TOTAL SCREEN TIME							

HOW DID YOU DO THIS WEEK?

Spending Screen Time

NAME
WEEK OF

DEVICES	MONDAY	TUESDAY	WEDNESDAY	THURSDAY	FRIDAY	SATURDAY	SUNDAY
CELL PHONE							
VIDEO GAMES							
TABLET							
KINDLE							
LAPTOP / COMPUTER							
TV							
TOTAL SCREEN TIME							

HOW DID YOU DO THIS WEEK?

Spending Screen Time

NAME	
WEEK OF	

DEVICES	MONDAY	TUESDAY	WEDNESDAY	THURSDAY	FRIDAY	SATURDAY	SUNDAY
CELL PHONE							
VIDEO GAMES							
TABLET							
KINDLE							
LAPTOP / COMPUTER							
TV							
TOTAL SCREEN TIME							

HOW DID YOU DO THIS WEEK?

Spending Screen Time

NAME	
WEEK OF	

DEVICES	MONDAY	TUESDAY	WEDNESDAY	THURSDAY	FRIDAY	SATURDAY	SUNDAY
CELL PHONE							
VIDEO GAMES							
TABLET							
KINDLE							
LAPTOP / COMPUTER							
TV							
TOTAL SCREEN TIME							

HOW DID YOU DO THIS WEEK?

Spending Screen Time

NAME		
WEEK OF		

DEVICES	MONDAY	TUESDAY	WEDNESDAY	THURSDAY	FRIDAY	SATURDAY	SUNDAY
CELL PHONE							
VIDEO GAMES							
TABLET							
KINDLE							
LAPTOP / COMPUTER							
TV							
TOTAL SCREEN TIME							

HOW DID YOU DO THIS WEEK?

Spending Screen Time

NAME	
WEEK OF	

DEVICES	MONDAY	TUESDAY	WEDNESDAY	THURSDAY	FRIDAY	SATURDAY	SUNDAY
CELL PHONE							
VIDEO GAMES							
TABLET							
KINDLE							
LAPTOP / COMPUTER							
TV							
TOTAL SCREEN TIME							

HOW DID YOU DO THIS WEEK?

Spending Screen Time

NAME	
WEEK OF	

DEVICES	MONDAY	TUESDAY	WEDNESDAY	THURSDAY	FRIDAY	SATURDAY	SUNDAY
CELL PHONE							
VIDEO GAMES							
TABLET							
KINDLE							
LAPTOP / COMPUTER							
TV							
TOTAL SCREEN TIME							

HOW DID YOU DO THIS WEEK?

Spending Screen Time

NAME	
WEEK OF	

DEVICES	MONDAY	TUESDAY	WEDNESDAY	THURSDAY	FRIDAY	SATURDAY	SUNDAY
CELL PHONE							
VIDEO GAMES							
TABLET							
KINDLE							
LAPTOP / COMPUTER							
TV							
TOTAL SCREEN TIME							

HOW DID YOU DO THIS WEEK?

Spending Screen Time

NAME	
WEEK OF	

DEVICES	MONDAY	TUESDAY	WEDNESDAY	THURSDAY	FRIDAY	SATURDAY	SUNDAY
CELL PHONE							
VIDEO GAMES							
TABLET							
KINDLE							
LAPTOP / COMPUTER							
TV							
TOTAL SCREEN TIME							

HOW DID YOU DO THIS WEEK?

Spending Screen Time

NAME							
WEEK OF							

DEVICES	MONDAY	TUESDAY	WEDNESDAY	THURSDAY	FRIDAY	SATURDAY	SUNDAY
CELL PHONE							
VIDEO GAMES							
TABLET							
KINDLE							
LAPTOP / COMPUTER							
TV							
TOTAL SCREEN TIME							

HOW DID YOU DO THIS WEEK?

Spending Screen Time

NAME	
WEEK OF	

DEVICES	MONDAY	TUESDAY	WEDNESDAY	THURSDAY	FRIDAY	SATURDAY	SUNDAY
CELL PHONE							
VIDEO GAMES							
TABLET							
KINDLE							
LAPTOP / COMPUTER							
TV							
TOTAL SCREEN TIME							

HOW DID YOU DO THIS WEEK?

Spending Screen Time

NAME	
WEEK OF	

DEVICES	MONDAY	TUESDAY	WEDNESDAY	THURSDAY	FRIDAY	SATURDAY	SUNDAY
CELL PHONE							
VIDEO GAMES							
TABLET							
KINDLE							
LAPTOP / COMPUTER							
TV							
TOTAL SCREEN TIME							

HOW DID YOU DO THIS WEEK?

Spending Screen Time

NAME:	
WEEK OF	

DEVICES	MONDAY	TUESDAY	WEDNESDAY	THURSDAY	FRIDAY	SATURDAY	SUNDAY
CELL PHONE							
VIDEO GAMES							
TABLET							
KINDLE							
LAPTOP / COMPUTER							
TV							
TOTAL SCREEN TIME							

HOW DID YOU DO THIS WEEK?

Spending Screen Time

NAME	
WEEK OF	

DEVICES	MONDAY	TUESDAY	WEDNESDAY	THURSDAY	FRIDAY	SATURDAY	SUNDAY
CELL PHONE							
VIDEO GAMES							
TABLET							
KINDLE							
LAPTOP / COMPUTER							
TV							
TOTAL SCREEN TIME							

HOW DID YOU DO THIS WEEK?

Spending Screen Time

NAME	
WEEK OF	

DEVICES	MONDAY	TUESDAY	WEDNESDAY	THURSDAY	FRIDAY	SATURDAY	SUNDAY
CELL PHONE							
VIDEO GAMES							
TABLET							
KINDLE							
LAPTOP / COMPUTER							
TV							
TOTAL SCREEN TIME							

HOW DID YOU DO THIS WEEK?

Spending Screen Time

NAME	
WEEK OF	

DEVICES	MONDAY	TUESDAY	WEDNESDAY	THURSDAY	FRIDAY	SATURDAY	SUNDAY
CELL PHONE							
VIDEO GAMES							
TABLET							
KINDLE							
LAPTOP / COMPUTER							
TV							
TOTAL SCREEN TIME							

HOW DID YOU DO THIS WEEK?

Spending Screen Time

NAME	
WEEK OF	

DEVICES	MONDAY	TUESDAY	WEDNESDAY	THURSDAY	FRIDAY	SATURDAY	SUNDAY
CELL PHONE							
VIDEO GAMES							
TABLET							
KINDLE							
LAPTOP / COMPUTER							
TV							
TOTAL SCREEN TIME							

HOW DID YOU DO THIS WEEK?

Spending Screen Time

NAME	
WEEK OF	

DEVICES	MONDAY	TUESDAY	WEDNESDAY	THURSDAY	FRIDAY	SATURDAY	SUNDAY
CELL PHONE							
VIDEO GAMES							
TABLET							
KINDLE							
LAPTOP / COMPUTER							
TV							
TOTAL SCREEN TIME							

HOW DID YOU DO THIS WEEK?

Spending Screen Time

NAME	
WEEK OF	

DEVICES	MONDAY	TUESDAY	WEDNESDAY	THURSDAY	FRIDAY	SATURDAY	SUNDAY
CELL PHONE							
VIDEO GAMES							
TABLET							
KINDLE							
LAPTOP / COMPUTER							
TV							
TOTAL SCREEN TIME							

HOW DID YOU DO THIS WEEK?

Spending Screen Time

NAME	
WEEK OF	

DEVICES	MONDAY	TUESDAY	WEDNESDAY	THURSDAY	FRIDAY	SATURDAY	SUNDAY
CELL PHONE							
VIDEO GAMES							
TABLET							
KINDLE							
LAPTOP / COMPUTER							
TV							
TOTAL SCREEN TIME							

HOW DID YOU DO THIS WEEK?

Spending Screen Time

DEVICES	MONDAY	TUESDAY	WEDNESDAY	THURSDAY	FRIDAY	SATURDAY	SUNDAY
NAME							
WEEK OF							

DEVICES	MONDAY	TUESDAY	WEDNESDAY	THURSDAY	FRIDAY	SATURDAY	SUNDAY
CELL PHONE							
VIDEO GAMES							
TABLET							
KINDLE							
LAPTOP / COMPUTER							
TV							
TOTAL SCREEN TIME							

HOW DID YOU DO THIS WEEK?

Spending Screen Time

NAME	
WEEK OF	

DEVICES	MONDAY	TUESDAY	WEDNESDAY	THURSDAY	FRIDAY	SATURDAY	SUNDAY
CELL PHONE							
VIDEO GAMES							
TABLET							
KINDLE							
LAPTOP / COMPUTER							
TV							
TOTAL SCREEN TIME							

HOW DID YOU DO THIS WEEK?

Spending Screen Time

NAME	
WEEK OF	

DEVICES	MONDAY	TUESDAY	WEDNESDAY	THURSDAY	FRIDAY	SATURDAY	SUNDAY
CELL PHONE							
VIDEO GAMES							
TABLET							
KINDLE							
LAPTOP / COMPUTER							
TV							
TOTAL SCREEN TIME							

HOW DID YOU DO THIS WEEK?

Spending Screen Time

NAME	
WEEK OF	

DEVICES	MONDAY	TUESDAY	WEDNESDAY	THURSDAY	FRIDAY	SATURDAY	SUNDAY
CELL PHONE							
VIDEO GAMES							
TABLET							
KINDLE							
LAPTOP / COMPUTER							
TV							
TOTAL SCREEN TIME							

HOW DID YOU DO THIS WEEK?

Spending Screen Time

NAME	
WEEK OF	

DEVICES	MONDAY	TUESDAY	WEDNESDAY	THURSDAY	FRIDAY	SATURDAY	SUNDAY
CELL PHONE							
VIDEO GAMES							
TABLET							
KINDLE							
LAPTOP / COMPUTER							
TV							
TOTAL SCREEN TIME							

HOW DID YOU DO THIS WEEK?

Spending Screen Time

NAME	
WEEK OF	

DEVICES	MONDAY	TUESDAY	WEDNESDAY	THURSDAY	FRIDAY	SATURDAY	SUNDAY
CELL PHONE							
VIDEO GAMES							
TABLET							
KINDLE							
LAPTOP / COMPUTER							
TV							
TOTAL SCREEN TIME							

HOW DID YOU DO THIS WEEK?

Spending Screen Time

NAME	
WEEK OF	

DEVICES	MONDAY	TUESDAY	WEDNESDAY	THURSDAY	FRIDAY	SATURDAY	SUNDAY
CELL PHONE							
VIDEO GAMES							
TABLET							
KINDLE							
LAPTOP / COMPUTER							
TV							
TOTAL SCREEN TIME							

HOW DID YOU DO THIS WEEK?

Spending Screen Time

NAME	
WEEK OF	

DEVICES	MONDAY	TUESDAY	WEDNESDAY	THURSDAY	FRIDAY	SATURDAY	SUNDAY
CELL PHONE							
VIDEO GAMES							
TABLET							
KINDLE							
LAPTOP / COMPUTER							
TV							
TOTAL SCREEN TIME							

HOW DID YOU DO THIS WEEK?

Spending Screen Time

NAME	
WEEK OF	

DEVICES	MONDAY	TUESDAY	WEDNESDAY	THURSDAY	FRIDAY	SATURDAY	SUNDAY
CELL PHONE							
VIDEO GAMES							
TABLET							
KINDLE							
LAPTOP / COMPUTER							
TV							
TOTAL SCREEN TIME							

HOW DID YOU DO THIS WEEK?

Spending Screen Time

NAME	
WEEK OF	

DEVICES	MONDAY	TUESDAY	WEDNESDAY	THURSDAY	FRIDAY	SATURDAY	SUNDAY
CELL PHONE							
VIDEO GAMES							
TABLET							
KINDLE							
LAPTOP / COMPUTER							
TV							
TOTAL SCREEN TIME							

HOW DID YOU DO THIS WEEK?

Spending Screen Time

NAME	
WEEK OF	

DEVICES	MONDAY	TUESDAY	WEDNESDAY	THURSDAY	FRIDAY	SATURDAY	SUNDAY
CELL PHONE							
VIDEO GAMES							
TABLET							
KINDLE							
LAPTOP / COMPUTER							
TV							
TOTAL SCREEN TIME							

HOW DID YOU DO THIS WEEK?

Spending Screen Time

NAME	
WEEK OF	

DEVICES	MONDAY	TUESDAY	WEDNESDAY	THURSDAY	FRIDAY	SATURDAY	SUNDAY
CELL PHONE							
VIDEO GAMES							
TABLET							
KINDLE							
LAPTOP / COMPUTER							
TV							
TOTAL SCREEN TIME							

HOW DID YOU DO THIS WEEK?

Spending Screen Time

NAME	
WEEK OF	

DEVICES	MONDAY	TUESDAY	WEDNESDAY	THURSDAY	FRIDAY	SATURDAY	SUNDAY
CELL PHONE							
VIDEO GAMES							
TABLET							
KINDLE							
LAPTOP / COMPUTER							
TV							
TOTAL SCREEN TIME							

HOW DID YOU DO THIS WEEK?

Spending Screen Time

NAME	
WEEK OF	

DEVICES	MONDAY	TUESDAY	WEDNESDAY	THURSDAY	FRIDAY	SATURDAY	SUNDAY
CELL PHONE							
VIDEO GAMES							
TABLET							
KINDLE							
LAPTOP / COMPUTER							
TV							
TOTAL SCREEN TIME							

HOW DID YOU DO THIS WEEK?

Spending Screen Time

NAME	
WEEK OF	

DEVICES	MONDAY	TUESDAY	WEDNESDAY	THURSDAY	FRIDAY	SATURDAY	SUNDAY
CELL PHONE							
VIDEO GAMES							
TABLET							
KINDLE							
LAPTOP / COMPUTER							
TV							
TOTAL SCREEN TIME							

HOW DID YOU DO THIS WEEK?

Spending Screen Time

NAME	
WEEK OF	

DEVICES	MONDAY	TUESDAY	WEDNESDAY	THURSDAY	FRIDAY	SATURDAY	SUNDAY
CELL PHONE							
VIDEO GAMES							
TABLET							
KINDLE							
LAPTOP / COMPUTER							
TV							
TOTAL SCREEN TIME							

HOW DID YOU DO THIS WEEK?

Spending Screen Time

NAME	
WEEK OF	

DEVICES	MONDAY	TUESDAY	WEDNESDAY	THURSDAY	FRIDAY	SATURDAY	SUNDAY
CELL PHONE							
VIDEO GAMES							
TABLET							
KINDLE							
LAPTOP / COMPUTER							
TV							
TOTAL SCREEN TIME							

HOW DID YOU DO THIS WEEK?

Spending Screen Time

NAME	
WEEK OF	

DEVICES	MONDAY	TUESDAY	WEDNESDAY	THURSDAY	FRIDAY	SATURDAY	SUNDAY
CELL PHONE							
VIDEO GAMES							
TABLET							
KINDLE							
LAPTOP / COMPUTER							
TV							
TOTAL SCREEN TIME							

HOW DID YOU DO THIS WEEK?

Spending Screen Time

NAME	
WEEK OF	

DEVICES	MONDAY	TUESDAY	WEDNESDAY	THURSDAY	FRIDAY	SATURDAY	SUNDAY
CELL PHONE							
VIDEO GAMES							
TABLET							
KINDLE							
LAPTOP / COMPUTER							
TV							
TOTAL SCREEN TIME							

HOW DID YOU DO THIS WEEK?

Spending Screen Time

NAME	
WEEK OF	

DEVICES	MONDAY	TUESDAY	WEDNESDAY	THURSDAY	FRIDAY	SATURDAY	SUNDAY
CELL PHONE							
VIDEO GAMES							
TABLET							
KINDLE							
LAPTOP / COMPUTER							
TV							
TOTAL SCREEN TIME							

HOW DID YOU DO THIS WEEK?

Spending Screen Time

NAME	
WEEK OF	

DEVICES	MONDAY	TUESDAY	WEDNESDAY	THURSDAY	FRIDAY	SATURDAY	SUNDAY
CELL PHONE							
VIDEO GAMES							
TABLET							
KINDLE							
LAPTOP / COMPUTER							
TV							
TOTAL SCREEN TIME							

HOW DID YOU DO THIS WEEK?